The Official
KOALA
HANDBOOK

The *Official*
KOALA
HANDBOOK

SIMON HUNTER

CHATTO & WINDUS
LONDON

Published in 1987 by Chatto & Windus Ltd,
30 Bedford Square, London WC1B 3RP,
by arrangement with Merehurst Ltd,
5 Great James Street, London WC1N 3DA.

British Library Cataloguing in Publication
Data, Hunter, Simon
  The official Koala handbook.
  I. Koalas
  1. Title
  599.2   QL737.M38

ISBN 0-7011-3213-2

Designed by Roger Daniels
Edited by Jenny Vaughan
Typeset by Lineage, Watford
Printed by New Interlitho S.p.A. Ltd, Italy
Typeset in 12/14 pt. Frutiger Light

ACKNOWLEDGEMENTS

The Author would like to thank the
management and staff of Taronga Zoo for
their help in preparing this book. In
particular, he would like to express his
gratitude to the Director, Jack Throp, for
his encouragement, and Dave Thomas,
section head of Australian mammals, who
inspired the author's special interest in
koalas, and was a great help in imparting
his vast knowledge of Australian mammals.

The Publishers would like to thank The
Australian Koala Foundation Inc. for their
help. The Foundation was set up in January
1986, with the aim of raising money to
encourage, co-ordinate and fund research
vital to the conservation of the koala.
If you would like more information,
contact: The Secretary, The Australian
Koala Foundation Inc., G.P.O. Box 346,
Brisbane, Queensland, Australia 4000.

CONTENTS

11/27/89

Koalas, the cuddliest of all Australian mammals, lead uneventful lives, high in their eucalyptus trees. Today's koalas are luckier than their ancestors, who were hunted first for food and then in larger numbers for their fur. But their future isn't altogether certain. Disease and loss of habitat threaten koalas, and they need our help if they are going to win through.

AN ODD CREATURE

This bas relief of a koala decorates the wall of a Melbourne country house, Burnham Beeches — now a hotel.

The koala is an odd creature that resembles in some respects several animals and consequently is known by various characteristic names: Australian bear, Australian sloth and Australian monkey. In a study of the animals on the great island it becomes apparent that in the process of evolution, if they evolved as claimed, some species must have been in doubt as to the next best form to assume, or element to live in and while in the throes of indecision have become fixed midway between bird and mammal, bear and monkey, a mere dubious thing of land, air and water but without a secure and positive habitat in either.

(From *Fur Trade of America* by A. L. Belden, 1917)

The koala, with its appealing face, big rubbery nose and large, fluffy ears, resembles a cuddly toy more than anything else. It has charmed generations of Australians and, since its first appearance on television, advertising Qantas, Australia's national airline, it has won hearts all over the world.

It is, of course, neither a bear nor a monkey, but a marsupial — a type of mammal that rears its young in a pouch and which is found mainly, but not exclusively in Australia. Its nearest living relative is the ground-dwelling wombat.

Despite the fact that it is very commonly known as the koala 'bear', or 'native bear', even a brief examination of its looks and lifestyle reveals that it is really most unlike any member of the bear family. Apart from its size (which is a fraction of that of even the smallest of bears) there is the question of its diet. Bears are usually omnivorous, eating almost anything, while koalas, whose diet is restricted to only a few kinds of eucalyptus, could hardly be less so.

The koala's bright eyes and puzzled expression have always appealed to human imagination — but its apparent sagacity is probably an illusion. Nor is it as cuddly as it seems; it has very sharp claws and smells strongly of eucalyptus.

Nevertheless, its appearance is so delightful that pictures of koalas and sometimes even live animals themselves have been used to encourage us to buy, among other things, cold drinks, dressing gowns, jelly crystals, paint, boot polish and (most famously) airline tickets.

Koalas have been reproduced by the million as toys — some, sadly, at the expense of (legally culled) kangaroos, from whose skins they are made, while others are fake-fur products. They have appeared on stamps, badges, plates and mugs, and have turned up countless times in children's books and comic strips — and not just in Australia. For although only a handful have ever left their homeland, they have endeared themselves to people everywhere.

The koala's apparent sagacity is probably an illusion,

but there is no
doubt that it has an
infinite capacity to
charm.

'LARGER THAN A WAUMBAT'

The first record of a koala being seen by a European dates from 26 January 1798. John Price, a young free servant of the then governor, Captain John Hunter, was travelling in the table lands west of Sydney, near the present town of Bargo, when he wrote in his diary of 'an animal which the natives call a Cullawine, which resembles the sloths of America'.

In 1802 an explorer, Ensign F. Barrallier, recorded that he had swapped a tomahawk and spears for the feet of an animal the Aboriginals told him was called a 'colo'. It was thought at the time to be a kind of monkey.

On 21 August the following year, the *Sydney Gazette* published the first detailed account of a koala. It describes an animal that Barrallier had captured and given to Governor King and, interestingly, shows an early appreciation of the koala's similarity to the wombat, and its limited choice of food.

'An animal whose species was never before found in the colony is in His Excellency's possession. When it was taken, it had two pups, one of which died a few days since. This creature is somewhat larger than a Waumbut, nevertheless, it differs from that animal. The fore and hind legs are of about equal length, having sharp talons at each of the extremities, with which it must have climbed the highest trees with much facility. The fur that covers it is soft and fine, and of a mixed grey colour; the ears are short and open; the graveness of the visage ... would seem to indicate more than an ordinary portion of animal sagacity. ... The surviving pup generally clings to the back of the mother, or is caressed with a serenity that appears peculiarly characteristic; it has a fake belly like the opossum; and the food consists of gum leaves, in the choice of which it is excessively nice.'

In 1816 the French naturalist de Blainville gave the koala its generic (or scientific) name, *Phascolarctos*, from the Greek words for 'leather pouch' and 'bear'. Later, the German naturalist Goldfuss gave it the specific name *cinereus*,

Natural history artist Marianne North painted this on her second visit to Australia in 1880-81.

meaning 'ash-coloured', after the colour of the original specimen. All this is despite the fact that koalas are often brown and are not bears!

Scientists in the 19th century discarded the idea that the koala was related to the wombat, suggesting first that it belonged in the same family as another marsupial, the cuscus, and then, later, the ring-tail possum. But by 1921, opinion had come full circle. The wombat theory was reinstated and remains in favour today.

But evolution has taken the two animals in very different directions; the koala has a nomadic life among the trees, while the down-to-earth wombat remains firmly in its burrow.

Early naturalists were fascinated by the koala and had a number of theories as to its ancestry.

Phascolarctos fuscus.

THE VERY FIRST KOALA

In the very distant, prehistoric past, marsupials could have been found (had anyone been looking) in many parts of the world. Today, with the exception of opossums in the Americas, they are mostly confined to Australia, having elsewhere become extinct, along with hairy mammoths and giant sloths.

It is the pouch that makes the marsupials special, as it marks the most important difference between them and the much commoner placentals — mammals without pouches which exist all over the rest of the world. The two types of mammal became distinct about 100 million years ago, when dinosaurs roamed the earth.

Fossils found in Europe indicate that marsupials existed there up to about 20 million years ago, before dying out in the face of competition with the more advanced mammals. No marsupial fossils have been found in either Africa or Asia — which suggests they never existed there.

Scientists think that Australia's marsupials reached their present home from South America by way of Antartica. This was possible because, millions of years ago, the world's continents were arranged quite differently from the way they are today. South America, Antarctica and Australia were once all joined together in a mass we now refer to as Gondwanaland. Animals were able to travel overland from one part of this great continent to another.

Australia became isolated from the rest of the world about 45 million years ago, and between that time and now the processes of evolution went on. This resulted in a whole range of marsupials, unknown elsewhere, which includes such diverse creatures as tiny mouse- and mole-like animals as well as hefty and powerful red kangaroos. But among all these, only the wombat bears any similarity to the koala.

It seems that these two animals developed separately from a single ancestor about 40 million years ago. They are alike in that both have cheek pouches in which they can store food, and in the fact that in both the pouch in which the females carry their young opens 'backwards', with the entrance towards the tail. In most marsupials the opposite is the case; the kangaroo's pouch, for example, opens at the top, like a pocket. But these features apart, the resemblance between koalas and wombats is limited.

There were once several different kinds of koala — all but one of which have died out. The earliest known member of the family was a browser, which lived 15 million years ago. Evidence of a 'giant' koala, twice the size of its modern descendant, exists in fossils dating back more than 40 000 years.

Today's small, tree-dwelling koala is the only remaining member of what was once a whole family of animals.

Its closest relative is the wombat, which stays firmly at ground level or below.

THE KOALA BOY

This story was told long ago by the Aboriginal people of Australia. It explains why the koala must always be treated with respect.

There was once a child whose parents died, and who was left in the charge of cruel relatives who forbade him to drink the water they had collected from the creek. The child was forced to eat eucalyptus leaves, and he was thirsty most of the time.

One day, these relatives went off into the bush for the day to hunt for food. By an oversight, they left their water vessels in a place where the child could reach them. As soon as they were out of sight, he took the opportunity to drink his fill.

Then, thinking of what might happen when they returned, he had the foresight to take some full vessels and hang them among the branches of a small tree. After that, he climbed into the tree himself, and began to sing an ancient and magical song.

At once, the tree began to grow taller and taller until the boy was high above the forest floor.

At dusk, his relatives returned, tired and thirsty. They immediately looked for their water vessels, but they were nowhere to be seen. Then one of them caught sight of the child sitting in the tree, with the water vessels beside him.

The hunters became very angry, for they could not reach the water, and they knew the boy had tricked them. But they were clever people and spoke gently to the child, telling him they were sorry they had treated him badly and that, if he were only to come down and bring the water with him, they would be kind to him. The boy believed them and made his way down to the ground.

But straightaway his relatives set about him with sticks and stones, beating him until his body was quite soft. Mad with anger, they continued to beat him until at last a strange thing happened. The boy began to change. He became shorter, stockier, and covered with grey fur. He was a koala!

At once, he turned and ran up the tree again, far out of reach of his tormentors.

They, in turn, began to chop the tree down, hacking away at its trunk until it crashed to the ground, spilling the water vessels as it did so. The water poured down, flooding across the forest floor as a mighty creek, and the koala-boy disappeared for ever into the night.

Since that time, it has been forbidden for the Aboriginal people to break the koala's bones when they kill it. Though they may eat the animal, they may not skin it, and they must always treat its body with respect. If they do not, there is a danger that all the water in the land will dry up, and there will be a terrible drought.

'Koobor the Drought Maker' by Ainslie Roberts illustrates one of several ancient Aboriginal legends associating the koala with the theme of drought.

A koala and a kangaroo, seen together at sunset. This is the time of day when the koala is most active.

FINDING KOALAS

Australia had played host to both visitors and settlers from Europe for many years before there were any recorded observations of koalas. Even in the 18th century, it seems, they were not a common sight. Probably, one of the main reasons for this is their very restricted diet, made up entirely of certain types of eucalyptus leaves. These cannot always be easily found.

Koalas have had a turbulent history since those early days. Their numbers declined massively in the 19th and early 20th centuries, as a result of hunting, but have recovered since then. There are no reliable estimates of today's population, but experts believe there may be between 100 000 and 500 000 koalas.

Although hunting is now outlawed, koalas still face problems. As forests are cleared, it becomes harder for them to find food and, in addition, they are susceptible to disease.

The main groups living out of captivity are in eastern Australia, among the wild eucalyptus forests and woodlands that stretch from Cooktown in northern Queensland (about 15 degrees south) to south-western Victoria (38 degrees south). But even here, they are found only in pockets of suitable vegetation.

Koalas have been introduced into Western Australia, where they were not found naturally in the recent past. Small numbers were released on to Phillip and French Islands (Victoria) as long ago as 1870, and these have increased to such an extent that there is now a problem of overcrowding. For this reason, many of the koalas from these areas have been removed to places where there would otherwise be few or none.

One such area is South Australia, where koalas had been hunted to extinction by the 1930s. They had already been taken to Flinders Island (off the South Australian coast) in 1923. Since then, new koala colonies have been set up in eight areas of mainland South Australia.

Although there is only one species of koala, there are noticeable variations — to such a degree that koalas have been described as being of three races.

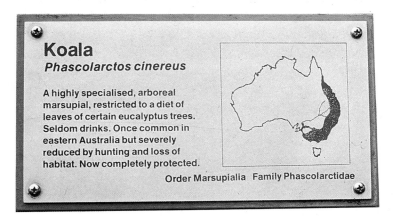

Koala
Phascolarctos cinereus

A highly specialised, arboreal marsupial, restricted to a diet of leaves of certain eucalyptus trees. Seldom drinks. Once common in eastern Australia but severely reduced by hunting and loss of habitat. Now completely protected.

Order Marsupialia Family Phascolarctidae

The shaggiest koalas, usually brown, are found in Victoria.

There is a grey or grey-brown koala, with ash-grey flecking, found mainly in New South Wales. Then there is a shorter-haired one, usually red or tawny in colour, which is found in Queensland. The third kind is found in Victoria, and has a sparser, shaggier coat of a more uniform brown. Generally, the ears of southern koalas tend to be fluffier than those of northern ones.

Koalas are smaller the further north they live; an average adult male in the north weighs about 6kg — only half the weight of his southern cousin. Head and body length together may range from 60 to 80cm. Females are usually smaller than males.

Queensland koalas
have the shortest
hair and the least
fluffy ears.

Koalas in New
South Wales tend to
be grey or
grey-brown.

EXCESSIVELY NICE

Koalas spend almost all their lives among the branches of eucalyptus trees. Most of the time they are asleep, wedged in the fork of a tree for safety. They are most wide awake at dusk, which is when they do most of their eating — about one and a half to two hours after sunset. But they do eat during the day as well, and can often be seen munching quietly away at their leaves.

As the *Sydney Gazette* noted in 1803, their taste in food is 'excessively nice'. They eat just a few species of eucalyptus, and sometimes nibble at forest oak and brush box. An adult koala will eat about half to three quarters of a kilogram of leaves (about half a dozen branches) in a 24-hour period.

There are 500-600 species of eucalyptus in Australia today, but of these, koalas are known to eat only about 50 or 60. A koala may confine itself to only two or three varieties, or may eat up to twelve depending on what is available in the area where it lives. It is extremely fussy and finds it difficult to adjust to a new variety, preferring to travel quite a long distance to find the leaf of its choice.

Eucalyptus leaves are rather an odd choice of food, as they contain oil and toxic chemicals which are harmful to most mammals. The amount of these substances in the

Eucalyptus leaves are tough, fibrous and poisonous to most mammals. They are the koala's only food.

leaves varies according to the time of year.

The oil contains *cineole*, which is poisonous to most mammals because it kills the bacteria in their gut. The bacteria in the koala's gut can resist its effects, it seems, even in the case of the manna gum which contains three times as much oil as most other leaves and is one of the commonest kinds of southern eucalyptus.

The oil does koalas no harm, but it does not seem to make the leaves especially desirable either, and koalas show no special preference for leaves with a high oil content.

The other poisonous substance in eucalptus is *hydrocyanic* (also known as *prussic*) acid, which can

A koala must take care when eating as some young shoots are poisonous.

be at lethal levels in new shoots. This helps the tree protect itself from being devastated by koalas after a bush fire, when it has just begun to grow new leaves and is especially vulnerable.

A careless koala eating these shoots could become very sick, or even die. It avoids this fate by taking great care over its food, pulling each branch towards its nose and giving each leaf a good sniff before beginning to nibble it — just to make sure it really is as good to eat as it looks.

Eating so much eucalyptus makes the koala smell rather strongly of eucalyptus oil — a fact that may deter many a would-be koala-cuddler.

Its rubbery nose is very sensitive, and the koala knows at once when leaves are fit to eat.

DRINK, DOPE AND DOZING

One of the most abiding myths about koalas is that they spend their entire life 'stoned' on eucalyptus oil. It is easy to understand how this idea came about. After all, for much of the time, they are almost immobile, dozing in tranquillity, high up in the trees.

But koalas are not in a permanent drugged stupor. It is just that they sleep when they have nothing else to do — which is most of the time, and at least 18 hours out of each 24. In zoos, where their food arrives without any effort on their part, they can be even more dozy.

Closer to reality, but nevertheless a myth, is the widely-held belief that koalas do not drink. It is even said that the name 'koala' comes from an Aboriginal word meaning 'I do not drink'.

But koalas do drink, and their name is probably simply a mispronunciation of the one the Aboriginal people gave them, which had no special meaning, any more than 'cat' or 'dog' have in English.

It is true, though, that koalas do not often need to seek out water on the ground, as the leaves they eat contain about 67 per cent water, not to mention the dew or raindrops on them. Koalas have little need of extra fluid, but those that live in dry areas, where leaves contain less moisture, may need to

Koalas are known to drink water on occasions ... but never champagne!

look for water. This also applies to old and sick koalas and nursing mothers.

A koala looking for water will, of course, have to climb down from its tree to find it. Once on the ground, it takes the opportunity to eat a little soil, which provides important minerals it needs to grow.

Soil aside, the koala's main source of nourishment remains the very tough and fibrous eucalyptus leaves. Its digestive system is well adapted to deal with them. Like other herbivores (plant-eaters) the koala has a special organ called the caecum which plays an important part in digesting food. But in most animals, this is quite small, measuring only about 10 per cent

Much of the koala's day is spent dozing. It sleeps for up to 18 hours out of 24.

Appearances are deceptive – a koala much prefers the fork of a tree to a bed.

of the body length. In the koala, the caecum is two metres long — twice as long as the koala itself! It is this extra-long digestive system which helps the koala break down its exceptionally tough food.

The koala cannot live anywhere where there is no eucalyptus to eat, and although these trees have been exported to many parts of the world, they have been mainly used for timber and firewood, not as potential koala-fodder.

It is only comparatively recently that a few foreign zoos — in the United States and Japan — have been able to provide enough of the right kinds of leaves to take on the responsibility of caring for expatriate koalas.

UP A GUM TREE

Koalas are superbly adapted to life in trees. They have an excellent sense of balance and some of the time do not even need to grip the branches among which they live — though they can do so at a moment's notice, if there is a risk of becoming unsteady.

They are great climbers, partly because of their especially strong thigh muscles, which are much lower down the shin than in most other mammals. The position of these muscles makes koalas slower but much better climbers than many other animals — 'slow but sure'.

Koalas stay in their trees in all sorts of weather: in the pouring rain, in fierce gales and in burning sunshine. They do not make any sort of shelter, but they have extra-thick fur on their shoulders and the backs of their necks to protect them from the worst of the weather. They do not sweat, but they can keep cool by licking their forearms and by stretching out as they rest in the trees.

Their hands and feet are also well adapted to their way of life. The first two digits on each hand are opposed to the others, creating the effect of two 'thumbs' and three 'fingers'. These, combined with very strong claws, give the koala a very powerful grip.

On the feet, there is only one 'thumb'. The second and third toes are joined, so that the claws are

The two thumbs on the koala's hands make a powerful clamp, and the rough pads and strong claws on both hands and feet help the koala to grip.

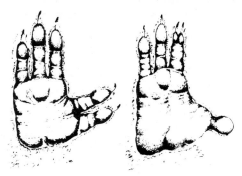

close enough together to act as a comb when the koala is grooming itself.

Koalas have granular pads on the soles of their feet and on the palms of their hands. These help them grip on to trees as they climb, and cushion them as they land when they jump from tree to tree, or from a tree to the ground.

For although they are mainly tree-dwellers, koalas are quite agile on the ground. They climb downwards in the way that they find easiest: backwards, bottom first. On the forest floor, they walk on all fours and although they appear quite awkward in that position, they are in fact able to get along fairly quickly.

Koalas climb down
a tree backwards,
bottom first.

Once on the ground
they look ungainly,
but they can move
quite fast.

Usually, a koala comes down from one tree in order to look for another. The koala may be a young male, out to set up a new territory for himself, or it may be hungry and looking for more food.

This is when the koala's exceptionally acute sense of smell comes into its own. The rubbery-looking nose, covered with fine hairs, is so sensitive that all the koala has to do is sniff the trunk of a eucalyptus tree and it can tell straightaway whether or not it is the sort it prefers to eat.

If the wandering koala judges the tree suitable, it will make its way upwards — climbing hand-over-hand, with care and determination.

FAMILY TREES

Koalas are usually thought of as solitary animals. In fact, they tend to live in loose-knit groups in areas of suitable trees.

Within these groups, there does not seem to be any special order of importance. For most of the year, the koalas will live happily and peacefully together as long as there are plenty of leaves. But during the breeding season, it quickly becomes clear that there is a dominant male.

If a family of koalas gets through all the leaves on its trees, they have no choice but to look for new ones. When this happens, the dominant male will usually leave the area first, with the females and the juvenile males setting out a few days later.

They do not all stay with the male. Some settle with him in the new area he has found, but others may go in different directions and find feeding-places for themselves, or join other groups of koalas.

Once settled in their new area, the koalas do not live very close to one another. Two koalas will rarely sleep or eat in the same tree, though a koala will take no notice at all of the other animals around it: the possums, gliders and birds of the bush.

During the breeding season (November to February in the south, September to January further north) the dominant male will exert his authority.

This is the time of year when

koalas prove themselves to be among the noisiest of all marsupials. The male begins by calling out, making a deep, grunting sound, a bellow, which not only attracts females but also warns other males to stay away. A female who is ready for mating will answer back.

The calling gets more intense and louder as the male gets more excited. At the same time, he claims his territory by grasping the base of a tree with his front feet and rubbing it with his chest. His scent gland is located in the skin of the chest, and it releases a very strong, musky odour which, like the calling, attracts females and

serves as a warning to other males.

Females also make a grunting noise, similar to the males, but not so loud. In addition, they will wail or scream if they are being attacked.

In times of stress, young koalas make a high-pitched squeal, like the sound of a young baby. This fact was emphasised by people campaigning for their protection. Koala hunting was always unpopular with animal-lovers. But when they discovered that a wounded young koala cries like a child, many people began to think of it in terms of murder.

A koala usually sleeps alone, rarely sharing its tree with another koala.

A young koala surveys its surroundings. If it is a male it will eventually leave home and search for new territory.

A TURBULENT LOVE-LIFE

Female koalas are mature by the time they are two years old, but a male must wait until he is three or four before he is ready to stake out a territory for himself and to look for a mate. A young mature male has to show a fair amount of determination and aggression in order to attract a female and mate with her. He will almost certainly have to do battle, right from the start.

When two males are attracted by the same female, the ensuing brawl can be very fierce — unless, of course, one of the males has heeded the warning given out in the bellowing and grunting of the other as he defends his territory. Fighting consists of savage bouts of biting, wrestling and chasing until one animal backs down.

Females live within territory that has been climbed by the dominant male in their group, and do not claim any for themselves. But they are nonetheless capable of being quite aggressive. A female may inflict severe injuries on any male that tries to mate with her when she does not want him to.

Mating usually happens at night. The female grips an upright branch while the male mounts her. He holds on to the same branch and grasps the back of her neck with his jaws. Although he may bellow both before and after mating, he is usually quiet during the event, as is the female.

Copulation itself takes only about one and a half minutes. This may be an adaptation to the koala's lofty environment — it is not always easy to be sure of a secure foothold high up among the eucalyptus branches!

A male koala may mate with up to six females during the breeding season; the exact number depends on how many females there are in his territory.

Pregnancy lasts for only 35 days, after which the young koala is born. During the birth, the koala sits on a large branch, with her back up against a tree trunk and her head bent slightly forwards. Red fluid is first ejected from her cloaca — the single opening marsupials have both for mating and for passing out waste products. A few minutes later, the tiny new-born koala appears.

It is pink, hairless, semi-transparent, streaked with blood and glistening wet. This minute creature, only about 19 millimetres long and weighing less than half a gram, then begins a monumental journey, climbing laboriously through its mother's fur to reach her pouch.

Fifteen to 20 minutes after giving birth, the female climbs the tree and starts feeding again.

A young koala's first forays out of its mother's pouch are short. It returns frequently for food and security.

A young koala well on the way to maturity. From a birth-weight of only 0.5g it may eventually reach 13kg.

BRINGING UP BABY

At birth, the young koala is at a very early stage of development. Its eyes and ears are sealed, and its mouth and nostrils are no more than rudimentary holes. But its forearms are strong enough for the tiny creature to use them to climb through its mother's fur and into her pouch.

Once inside, the 'joey' (young koalas share this name with infant kangaroos) attaches itself to one of its mother's two teats. One of these may already be enlarged from feeding an older brother or sister, who will have left the pouch by now. The newcomer clamps its mouth around the other teat.

Very young koalas hold on to the teat so firmly that when early naturalists tried to pull a young koala out of its mother's pouch, they tore the skin from the joey's gums as they prized them from the teat, making the mouth bleed. From this the naturalists mistakenly concluded that this meant the young koala was actually organically attached to the teat, growing from it as if it were a fruit on a tree.

The koala's pouch remains at the right temperature and humidity for the young, whatever the conditions outside. The developing koala remains there for five-and-a-half months before venturing out.

Its first forays into daylight are short, and it returns quite quickly for food and security. The mother is

Hand rearing a koala isn't easy — but this one seems to have mastered the feeding-bottle.

A young koala clings to its mother's back after it has left the pouch. It is not weaned until it is a year old.

able to use these periods to lick clean the inside of her pouch.

At six months, the young koala is about 19cm long, weighs about 300-500 grams and is fully furred. During the next couple of months it ventures out of the pouch for longer and longer periods, but goes back in to sleep or if it is in danger.

At eight months it is permanently out of the pouch, clinging to its mother's back or stomach and only sticking its head back inside to drink. It is at this stage a mother may be seen with two young — suggesting that she has twins. In fact, twins are very rare and the second joey is usually one that has been adopted for some reason.

At twelve months, the young koala is weaned. During the process of weaning, it will eat digested gum leaves, which its mother passes out of her body through her cloaca. This food contains the bacteria which the young koala needs to develop in its own digestive system, so that it can break down these leaves for itself.

As they mature, female koalas tend eventually to leave their mothers and go looking for new areas to live and attach themselves to other males. The young males get chased away from their home by the dominant male during the breeding season and when they are four or five years old, will eventually try to claim their own territory elsewhere.

At seven or eight months, the joey is permanently out of the pouch.

FACING THE ENEMY

Koalas are thought to live for about twelve to fourteen years in the wild, and they have been known to survive in captivity until they are about sixteen or seventeen. But any wild animal is likely to have its life cut short by predators, disease and other dangers, and the koala is no exception.

The koala's main enemies are the dingo and the fox. Neither of these can attack while it remains aloft in a eucalyptus tree, but the koala is at great risk from predators when it decides to move from one tree to another. However, a healthy, strong, adult koala can put up quite a fight in self-defence. It will back up to a tree and strike out with its sharp claws, often inflicting severe damage on its attacker.

If the predator can be distracted for just a second, the koala will turn and leap up the tree in a series of upward jumps until it is out of danger. After that, it will use a hand-over-hand method of climbing to reach its eating or sleeping place.

Eventually, it will have to return to the ground in order to continue its interrupted journey. Coming down feet first gives it an advantage, as it can easily leap back up the tree if the danger appears once again.

Old, sick and young koalas are the most vulnerable when they are on the ground. They are weaker and move more slowly, and so find

Despite its cuddly image, the koala can be quite aggressive when provoked.

it difficult either to fight or make an escape.

The young have other enemies too: the wedge-tailed eagle will snatch any it sees on the ground, while powerful owls can pick them out of trees. Adults, however, are quite safe from predators while they are in their trees.

Predators are not the only danger. Natural disasters present serious threats. Fire is one of the greatest hazards; it is both common and devastating in the koala's bushland home. As the flames sweep through the trees, the koala's chances of survival are small, whether it stays in its tree or attempts to get to the ground and away.

Forest fires are one of the greatest hazards facing koalas. Escape is difficult, and injuries can result in a slow and painful death.

If it does survive the heat of the fire, any burns the koala sustains can easily become infected by flies laying their eggs in the wounds, making healing impossible and a slow death the likely result.

Koalas stand a much better chance in floods. They are strong, though clumsy, swimmers and move laboriously through the water with almost their whole body submerged.

Koalas are at their most vulnerable when they are on the ground. There, they may fall prey to the wedge-tailed eagle (right) or the dingo (above).

SAVE THE KOALA!

Inevitably, the koala's most destructive enemy has been mankind. During the 1860s, the koala began to be hunted for its fur, and this continued until the late 1920s.

By the end of the 19th century, the trade had become massive, with between 10 000 and 30 000 skins reaching the main market in London each year.

There they fetched between fivepence and a shilling apiece — a pittance, even in those days. Koala fur was considered useful because it was cheap and durable.

Mass slaughter went on for many years, although it was clear to most wildlife experts that koalas could not possibly survive such an onslaught. In 1919, a million skins were sold in Queensland alone and, in 1924, another million koalas were slaughtered in New South Wales.

This carnage took place despite the fact that protective legislation existed in most states by the beginning of the 20th century. Koala-hunting was outlawed in Victoria, for example, in 1898, and in Queensland in 1906. But poaching went on, and unknown numbers of koala skins were sent abroad labelled 'wombat'. In Queensland there was another problem. Although koalas were supposed to be protected, there was a series of 'open seasons' when they could be killed.

A trailer-load of koala-skins in the 1920s. Despite protective legislation, they were killed in massive numbers.

One of these was in 1927 when, following reports of excessive overpopulation, the Queensland Government declared August 'open'. In that single month, more than 600 000 koala skins were sold by hunters. The first few days of August saw thousands upon thousands of furs delivered for processing, with all the hunters claiming that nothing had been shot before 1 August!

The late 1920s saw the formation of the Wildlife Preservation Society of Australia, which was determined to put a stop to the trade in koala fur.

Campaigning included a direct approach to the President of the United States, to point out that koala skins, usually labelled 'wombat', were being imported into North America in vast numbers.

Popular opinion won the day

Koalas today are often found in sanctuaries or reserves, where they have special protection.

The Australian Koala Foundation Inc. (formerly the Australian Koala Association) was set up in 1986.

Australians everywhere have begun to realise that koalas cannot survive without human help.

and, on 10 November 1927, the Commonwealth Government ceased altogether issuing permits for the export of koala furs.

Today, the koala is the subject of a considerable amount of legislation. In Queensland and Victoria it has the special status usually only given to animals that are on the verge of extinction — even though sanctuaries and reserves have ensured that koalas are not in immediate danger.

The koala is really very lucky. It has an enviable ability to charm its public, whose concern for its welfare has, at least so far, ensured its survival. After all, how could such an appealing little creature ever be allowed to die out?

NO PLACE LIKE HOME

The arrival of the Europeans at the end of the 18th century signalled the end of an era when the human population in Australia lived in some degree of harmony with the natural world.

Until they were themselves killed in large numbers and driven from their homes, the Aboriginal people apparently lived alongside koalas and hunted them for food. This kept koala numbers down and perhaps explains why it was some years after the first settlement before a koala was seen by a European. But nothing could compare with the devastating attack the settlers later made on koalas and all forms of wildlife. In addition to killing huge numbers of koalas for fur, the newcomers began to clear away the eucalyptus forest to make farmland — thus depriving koalas of their homes and food.

No one knows exactly how much of the forest has been cleared since the first European farmers began work on the land. The koala was threatened for so long by hunters that for many years it probably seemed that the disappearance of its trees was the least of its problems. But now the koala is protected by law, it is obvious that, if it is to survive, it must have somewhere safe to live.

The largest populations of koalas today live in a number of small, well-managed sanctuaries and

This koala's habitat was destined to be blasted away as a quarry expanded. Its removal was forceful, much resented, and very undignified.

reserves. Others are found in state forests and on private land. Outside reserves, they are always in danger of losing their homes, through logging in the forests and development of the land.

Most states have powers to acquire land if wildlife appears to be threatened. But powers are one thing, action is another. There may not be enough funds to buy land, or there may be political reasons for not doing so.

But, even if all the remaining eucalyptus forest could be preserved, the koala would still have problems. For the refuges and sanctuaries in which they live are small and are surrounded by large areas which are quite unsuitable for them. This means that if there are too many koalas in one place, it is almost impossible for them to leave. It is too dangerous for them to cross main roads, farmland or built-up areas and, as a result, the forest becomes overcrowded.

Food becomes scarce, disease spreads easily and, if there is a natural disaster such as a forest fire, there is simply nowhere for the survivors to go to.

Solving these problems must be a priority. It would be all too easy for koala numbers to reach a critical low point. Removing koalas from overcrowded areas, protecting existing forest, planting more food trees and researching into disease are all vital if the koala is to survive.

The koala has existed in Australia since the dawn of time, and appears in several Aborginal legends. But today, its survival depends on giving it the space it needs to live.

THE SECRET ENEMY

In spite of all the protection koalas get today, they are still in serious danger — from an insidious disease.

Until recently, koalas were thought to suffer from four common and unrelated diseases: conjunctivitis, which can lead to blindness; cysts of the ovaries, which can cause infertility in females; pneumonia; and a disease called 'dirty tail', the symptoms of which are clear from its name.

In the mid-1970s, an organism called *Chlamydia psittaci* was isolated from the eyes of blind koalas. Over the next ten years, scientists came to realise that this organism — usually just called Chlamydia — was responsible for all four of the main koala ailments.

Chlamydia is sexually transmitted, which makes it especially problematic, since the koala cannot attempt to reproduce without passing it on. It is more common among some groups of koalas than others. Some authorities think that it is most serious where the koala population is under pressure as a result of poor nutrition, overcrowding, confinement to restricted areas and the loss of its food trees. Disease inevitably spreads rapidly in these conditions.

Its effects appear to vary from place to place. For example, on Phillip Island, off the coast of Victoria, more than 90 per cent of

The koala's chief enemy is disease, and finding a cure is a priority. Singer John Williamson released this record in 1986, to raise money for research.

World attention has begun to be focused on the koala, as its plight becomes more widely known.

the koala population has Chlamydia and many are infertile. But few suffer from the conjuctivitis which is another symptom of infection.

Conjunctivitis appears quite often in areas of Queensland and New South Wales, where the koalas are quite fertile.

Studies on Phillip Island show that apart from infertility, the disease there has few ill-effects — the females actually seem to be fitter, since they do not have to give birth and rear young.

Fears for the koala's survival have led to a campaign to support research into Chlamydia, in the hope of finding treatment for it. The main difficulty is developing an

An infected koala, too weak to move or to find food.

antibiotic that does not kill off the bacteria in the gut, which the koala needs to digest its food. There have already been some hopeful signs, but research costs money, and fund-raising is important.

American Express launched a campaign in 1984, and in 1986 a hit song, 'Goodbye Blinky Bill', climbed high in the Australian charts, with one Australian dollar from the proceeds of each record going to Chlamydia research.

Such efforts are vital — not only to pay for research into disease, but to look into all aspects of koalas' lives, so that those populations of koalas that are still healthy and breeding well stay that way.

FIRST CATCH YOUR KOALA

Catching koalas is not easy! They are far more adept at moving around in a tree than their human pursuers can ever be. But they have to be captured now and again so that checks can be made on their health and welfare, or so that they can be moved from one area to another.

Koala-catchers use a long rope with a noose for lassoing the koala, attached to a six-metre aluminium pole. These are manipulated first to cajole and then to hoist the koala out of its tree and on to a tarpaulin held below. None of this pleases the koala very much. Not only does it wail piteously as it falls, but it also protests by spraying its captors with eucalyptus-scented urine.

Once at ground level, the koala is quickly bundled into a sack, where the darkness usually calms it down.

A frightened, angry koala has to be handled carefully, and catchers may wear thick gloves to protect themselves from its sharp teeth and claws. The team acts as fast as possible, weighing and measuring each koala, checking it for disease and taking swabs from its eyes. It is tagged, usually on the ear, before it is released.

If the koala is to be moved to another part of the country, it is packed firmly into a crate, along with a bunch of gum leaves. The time between capture and being set free is usually less than 24 hours, to keep stress to a minimum.

A koala must first be cajoled from its position high in a eucalpytus tree.

Koalas have to be moved when a group grows too large for its habitat, or when the forest where it is living is threatened. The natural thing for koalas to do in these circumstances is to move on — but in the modern world this is often impossible. So, for many years, conservationists have been coming to the aid of koalas.

Here, the island populations of koalas, such as those on Phillip and French Islands (Victoria) and on Kangaroo Island (South Australia) are typical. Confined by the ocean, and well protected by law, these groups have been invaluable in helping to repopulate other parts of Australia with koalas.

Although many koalas live wild

Now that it is
within reach, it can
be hooked to the
ground.

Once on the ground, a koala's weight can be recorded, and a tag is put in its ear.

in reserves, there are a large number living in the more controlled conditions of zoos and sanctuaries. Koalas do well in captivity as long as they have the right food.

But keeping koalas in a built-up area presents problems. The staff at Sydney's Taronga Zoo, for example, have to spend a great deal of time scouring the city for suitable eucalyptus trees and, with their owner's permission, cutting off branches. The koalas seem to appreciate this effort, and display a great deal of excitement (at least in koala terms) when their food is brought to them, sometimes making a grab for it as the keeper passes their enclosure.

IN-FLIGHT KOALAS

The fact that koalas have little history of long-distance travel may come as a surprise to television viewers the world over. We have become used to seeing them occupying first-class seats in aircraft, passing the time of day with celebrities, even lolling in hotel beds. Such behaviour is most unnatural, and has to be coaxed from koalas by various means.

Koalas have played a central part for nearly 20 years in promoting Australia's national airline, Qantas. The airline has chosen to represent the koala (probably fairly accurately) as a grumpy little creature. It first appeared in its promotional role in 1967, in the United States, when a star named Teddy made his television debut. Teddy was not an Australian, having been born in San Diego Zoo, and the advertisements he appeared in were filmed in America. Teddy died in 1976 and later commercials involved Australian settings and home-grown koalas.

Koalas do not make very easy film stars. They are difficult, if not impossible, to train — the best one can hope for is a koala that is used to being handled. But the advertisements call for koalas to perform in all sorts of ways. Their lips must move so that they appear to speak. They must raise their fists, turn around crossly to face a camera, walk along a prescribed route, sit in a boat and much more.

The secret of success very often lies in the judicious use of eucalyptus leaves. A koala moves its lips as it chews a leaf, and as long as the viewer cannot see any part of the leaf sticking out of its mouth, dubbing can be very convincing. (The koalas that first appeared on United States television seemed to speak with an American accent, as the promoters feared that an Australian one would not be easily understood by viewers.)

Another trick is to hold a bunch of eucalyptus leaves above the koala's head, out of sight of the camera. The koala will raise a hand to reach them, and careful filming

Koalas are difficult to train, and a camera crew must find ways of persuading a koala to perform for television.

can suggest that it is saluting. A koala can be made to take a route past a camera if it is given a trail of leaves to follow and an appetising-looking bunch to aim for.

Jangling keys behind its back can make it turn round and glare at the camera. To persuade it to lie in a hotel bed, a plank has to be put between the sheets, for koalas prefer hard surfaces.

Koala stars are treated with great care and respect. There is always at least one handler present during filming, whose job it is to decide what can be reasonably asked of a koala, and who will say when enough is enough for one day. No one has any objection to this — the film crews along with everyone else have a tendency to fall in love with these koala stars!

Qantas, Australia's national airline, has used the koala in its advertisements for many years. Several koalas have become 'stars' of the screen. They are usually shown as rather grumpy individuals.

THE MILLION-DOLLAR TRAVELLER

Whatever the advertisements suggest, travel for a koala is much more complicated than it is for us. Apart from the difficulties and stress it involves, there is always the problem that, wherever a koala goes, eucalyptus trees must have gone first.

Until 1980, it was forbidden to export koalas at all. For years, the only ones outside Australia were in San Diego Zoo, where they had been kept since 1915. The situation there was ideal, as eucalyptus trees had flourished in California since the previous century. A further shipment of

koalas followed in 1959, and in 1976 eight were sent to Los Angeles. These were Australia's gift to the United States, to mark the American bi-centennial celebrations.

The law changed in 1980, and regulations were drawn up about how koalas should be cared for before, during, and after travel abroad.

These came into effect in 1984, and at once there was a mini-boom in koala export to Japan. Koalas quickly won the hearts of the Japanese people, and Japanese zoos made the most careful preparations to receive them. Ten koalas have been exported to Japan since 1984.

TAMA ZOO, TOKYO

Ear tag colour: BLACK

Koalas have proved exceptionally popular in Japan, and several have been exported to Japanese zoos.

extensive. These included making sure that the eucalyptus trees growing in Japan were suitable.

Leaves were flown to Australia from Japan three weeks before the departure, so that the koalas were able to get used to their new food. Keepers at Taronga kept a close watch on the koalas to see which leaves they liked best and how much they ate. Japanese zoo keepers, horticulturalists and other staff also arrived, to learn all they could about koala-keeping.

Meanwhile, special boxes were being made in which to carry the koalas. Each had a forked branch for the animal to sit on during the trip. (Despite the advertisements, airline seats do not really suit

Sydney's Taronga Zoo was involved in the export of koalas to two Japanese zoos in 1984 and 1985. The event was planned well ahead, and preparations were

A Japanese koala enthusiast welcomes a new arrival.

koalas.) Once on board, the koalas were put in a quiet place, with their attendants nearby. On arrival, they were taken immediately to their new homes, where they were monitored 24 hours a day.

The koalas made news headlines when they arrived in Japan, and were greeted by crowds at the airport. One shipment was accompanied by a government minister and the Premier of Queensland. Such a reception may seem a little excessive for such small animals — though not if the price of their journey is anything to go by. One newspaper estimated that each little traveller cost about a million Australian dollars to send.

A koala settles in its new home – in the full glare of publicity.

KOALA CLASSICS

Norman Lindsay was one of Australia's best-known illustrators — and he is still famous for his koalas. They first appeared in the Australian magazine *The Bulletin* and a selection is shown below.

Lindsay's koalas really came into their own with his book *The Magic Pudding*, published in 1918. This featured one of the very first koala characters — Bunyip Bluegum, who has become an Australian folk-hero.

WEAR YOUR OWN FACE

"Now I wonder how THIS YEAR is going to turn out?"

Optimus Possum: "Going to be a great year. Believe me, things are going to hum."

"Smart fellow, Optimus, knows what he's talking about....."

Yet another Norman Lindsay bear appears in the foreword to A. B. 'Banjo' Paterson's book of children's poems, *The Animals Noah Forgot*. Paterson published this delightful collection of verse in 1933. Most of the poems feature Australian wildlife of one sort or another. There are no verses actually about koalas, but a 'native bear' appears in the foreword, explaining how koalas survived the Flood (which was not as high in Australia as elsewhere) by remaining at the tops of their gum trees and calling to Noah as the ark drifted by.

by A.B. Paterson ("Banjo")
illustrated by Norman Lindsay

Dorothy Wall's koala character, Blinky Bill, first appeared in print in 1933. Along with his partners in mischief, Splodge the Kangaroo and Wally the Wombat, he has been a favourite with Australian children for generations.

A Lansdowne Australian Classic

TWO THUMBS
the Koala

written by LESLIE REES
illustrated by MARGARET SENIOR

Two Thumbs the Koala, written by Leslie Rees, and illustrated by Margaret Senior, was first published in 1951. It had an unashamedly educational message, and was packed with information about the natural history of the koala.

As a vehicle for teaching about conservation it was, and still is, a huge success. 'Two Thumbs' is a very real koala, and like his modern descendants, he faces a whole series of problems as he survives a bush fire, the inept attentions of a well-meaning human family and a poacher's trap, before settling down in the protection of a sanctuary.

KOALAS IN THE NEWS

Koalas can have few complaints about press coverage. After all, they owe much to the media. In the 1920s, for example, the danger of their extinction was reported and campaigned against. More recently, the threat posed by Chlamydia has been relayed to the public both through newspapers and television programmes. All this plays a vital part in the koala's survival, since it makes raising extra money for research easier.

Koalas have also made news as symbols and mascots. When Teddy the first Qantas koala died, the event hit the headlines in the United States. In the early 1960s, another real-life koala, named Smokey, became a star in South Australia when he appeared on posters and on television in a publicity campaign against forest fires.

The arrival of koalas in Japan was greeted with a fanfare of media attention and crowds at the airport. There are reports that some people dressed as koalas for the occasion.

This overwhelming interest was a source of puzzlement to a great many Australians — not least among whom was probably John Brown, Australia's Federal Minister for Tourism. He had caused a furore in 1983 by publicly attacking the koala, saying that it stank, scratched, piddled on people and was covered with fleas.

These remarks made headlines.

Minister for Tourism John Brown tries to make friends with Narrumpi, a crochety koala, who responded by biting him.

Doubts were expressed as to whether it was appropriate to retain such an apparently unsavoury animal as Australia's Olympic team's mascot. Koalas seemed to be in danger of losing their status as Australia's most cuddly animal.

But newspapers, opposition politicians and even the Prime Minister quickly leaped to the koala's defence. Outrage at Mr Brown's comments was expressed in all quarters. The press was bombarded with letters from koala-lovers and newspapers responded by printing numerous photographs of some of the millions of people, including royalty, who had publicly cuddled koalas and had emerged both dry and unscathed.

Eighteen months later, the remarks were still remembered and there were delighted reports of the koala's revenge. The same Mr Brown was asked to open a new koala compound at Healesville Sanctuary, near Melbourne, where he apologised for his earlier remarks and assured the public that no malice had been intended.

The apology was not accepted. Mr Brown tried to make his peace with the species by scratching a koala named Narrumpi on the head. Narrumpi, whose temper had been spoiled by injuries sustained in a bushfire, would have none of it. He bit Mr Brown in the stomach.

Princess Diana sports a koala knitted into her sweater ... but

Princess Alexandra has the chance to meet the real thing.

WHERE TO SEE KOALAS

OUTSIDE AUSTRALIA

Koalas can be seen in the following zoos outside Australia:

San Diego Zoo, PO Box 551, San Diego, California, CA 92112, U.S.A.;

Los Angeles Zoo, 5333 Zoo Drive, Los Angeles, California, CA 90027, U.S.A.;

San Fransisco Zoological Gardens, Zoo Road, and Skyline Boulevard, San Francisco, California, CA 94132, U.S.A.;

Tama Zoological Park, Hodokubo, Hinoshi, Tokyo, Japan;

Higashiyama Zoological Park, Higashiyama Motomachi, Chikusa-ku, Nagoya-shi, Aichi-ken, Japan;

Hirakawa Zoological Park, Hirakawa-cho, Kagoshima-shi, Kagoshima-ken, Japan.

AUSTRALIA

The following is a list of places where koalas can be seen at close quarters:

Queensland

Lone Pine Sanctuary, Jesmond Road, Fig Tree Pocket, Queensland, 4069. (11 km south of Bisbane.) Visitors can hear a talk about koalas while they are in the koala enclosure, and are allowed to cuddle the koalas and have their picture taken while they do so.

Currumbin Sanctuary, 28 Tomewin Street, Currumbin, Queensland 4223. (Gold Coast.) Koalas can be seen in natural bushland at close quarters from several levels. They cannot be handled or touched, but they are fed twice a day and a talk is given during the feeding.

Alma Park Zoo, Alma Road, Kallangur, Queensland 4503. (28 km north of Brisbane.) Visitors can walk through the koala's enclosure and can hold koalas if they ask to do so.

New South Wales

Taronga Zoo,
PO Box 20, Mosman,
N.S.W. 2088.
The zoo is in a dramatic setting overlooking Sydney Harbour. The koalas are housed in a circular building which allows viewing from ground level to tree-top levels. They cannot be touched or handled.

Featherdale Wildlife Park,
217 Kildare Road, Doonside, N.S.W. 2767. (35 km west of Sydney.)
Koalas here can be handled and photographed twice a day.

Waratah Park,
Namba Road, Terrey Hills, New South Wales, 2084. (15 km north of Sydney.)
The koalas are kept in a bush setting, through which visitors can walk. This is open hourly, and the animals can be touched and photographed.

Koala Park, Castle Hill Road, West Pennant Hills, New South Wales 2120. (25 km north of Sydney.)
The koalas are kept in a bushland setting and are fed twice daily — during which time they can be handled and photographed.

Western Plains Zoo,
Obley Road, Dubbo, New South Wales 2830.
The koalas are kept in one acre of natural bushland. Visitors can walk through this, but they cannot handle the koalas.

Victoria
Royal Melbourne Zoo, Elliot Avenue, Parkville, Victoria 3052.
The koalas are kept in enclosures with a low barrier. They cannot be touched or handled.

Healesville,
Badger Creek Road, Victoria 3777. (65 km east of Melbourne.)
The koalas are kept in enclosures with a low barrier, and can be handled at various times during the year.

Creswick Park,
Creswick, Victoria 3363. (100 km west of Melbourne.)
This is an area of bushland set aside for the breeding of koalas from the surrounding forest. They can be seen in various trees throughout the park, but cannot be handled.

Phillip Island, Cowes, Victoria, 3922. (90 km south of Melbourne.) Areas of this island are set aside for koalas. They can be seen in their natural habitat, and cannot be touched or handled.

South Australia

Adelaide Zoo, Frome Road, Adelaide, South Australia 5000. The koalas are kept in open, natural exhibits where they can be easily seen, but cannot be handled.

Cleland Conservation Park, Sumertown, South Australia 5141. (18 km south-east of Adelaide.) Koalas can be seen each afternoon, and can be held and photographed if the conditions permit.

Western Australia

Yanchep National Park, Yanchep, Western Australia 6035. (50 km north of Perth.) Koalas are kept in walk-through enclosures and can be seen during the day eating and sleeping in large gum trees. They cannot be handled or touched.

Perth Zoo, 20 Labouchere Road, South Perth, Western Australia 6151. Koalas are kept in an open exhibit where they can be easily seen, but cannot be handled.

A.C.T.

Rehwinkels Animal Park, Macks Reef Road, Sutton, ACT 2620. (24 km east of Canberra.) The koalas are in an enclosure, where they can be seen at close quarters.

Tidbinbilla Nature Reserve, Tharwa, ACT 2620. (40 km west of Canberra.) Koalas can be seen in a natural, bushland setting, but cannot be handled or touched. There is a map at the park entrance, which shows visitors where koalas have most recently been spotted.

Koalas also inhabit a number of National Parks and Reserves within their range, where they are totally protected.

The koala enclosure at Taronga Zoo, Sydney.

DID YOU KNOW?

A koala back-pack. It could almost be the real thing.

Expensive tastes

It seems that koalas have a taste for money. In 1983, a koala named Clinker was present at a ceremony at the Royal Botanic Gardens in Sydney, when the Kimberly Clark industrial group presented a cheque for 50 000 Australian dollars to the World Wildlife Fund. The company made the mistake of using a gimmick: the cheque was printed on a eucalyptus leaf. Clinker could think of better uses for it than banking it. He seized it and ate it.

The firm replaced the cheque.

Koala travellers

There is an unlikely story that a koala found its way to Scotland with a sailor in the early 1800s, and was returned to Australia at the end of the visit. The first authenticated instance of a koala leaving its native land was in 1880, when London Zoo in Regent's Park acquired one. It was given very special care, but sadly it lived for only 14 months. One night, it fell into a washstand and suffocated.

Foster-mother

It is illegal to keep koalas as pets, and has been so for many years. But exceptions have been made. In 1937, Mrs Oswin Roberts of Cowes on Phillip Island, Victoria, reared a young orphan she called Edward. He slept in a cot, and joined the family for meals, sitting in a child's high-chair as he nibbled eucalyptus leaves. As a young koala, he enjoyed sitting on her head as she went about her garden.

Up the pole
Occasionally, koalas are seen to climb up telephone poles. Amusing as this may look, the reasons are rather sad. Koalas become confused if their habitat is destroyed, and may be driven to climb quite unsuitable objects.

A tight fit
Koala twins are rare. There has been only one known instance of them being born. This was in 1965, at West Burleigh Fauna Reserve, in Queensland. They were discovered in their mother's pouch, and were still both very young when they grew too large to remain in there together. Staff say that it would have been impossible for them both to fit in, even with the help of a shoe horn! The little animals were hand-nursed alternately, giving each a chance to spend some time in the pouch while the other was kept warm outside it.

On your bike
In 1980, a koala named Cuthbert from a colony near Melbourne became attracted to the noise of a motorbike and eventually took the occasional ride on it, seated on the pillion and holding firmly on to the machine's owner.

Confused, a disorientated koala clings to a telegraph pole.

Gumlypta, agricultural chemicals, used a koala motif in 1919.

An undated advertisement for jelly crystals relies on the name of the koala alone.

The Perdriau Rubber Company's koala symbol, 1916. It was used to sell medicine.

These are musical koalas – the trademark of Lewis Ornstien's sound records in 1958.

'Bear Brand' pots and kettles took up the koala theme in 1947.

Dr Blue Gum, promoting eucalyptus oil in 1916.

J. M. Baker's mineral waters used the koala in their trademark in 1945.

Koala memorabilia has always been popular. Right: a money box, guarded by a Blinky Bill lookalike. Far right: the koala's rotund figure reproduced as a teapot. Below: a puzzle for young children, designed by George Luck.

PICTURE CREDITS 59 (top), Australian Koala Foundation Inc.; 1, 82 (left), Australia Post; 87 (left), Jim Bennett, Camera Press; 33 (left), 46, 48, 57, 66, 67, Steve Brown; 59 (bottom), Don Burnett; 37 (bottom), Tanya Clayton; 42, 43, Colour Library Books Limited; 53, 61 87 (right), Pictures reproduced by courtesy The Courier-Mail, Brisbane, Australia; 95 (right), The Covent Garden General Store, London WC2; 95 (lower left), Design Council Picture Library/Design Selection Magazine; 63, 'Didane the Koala' by G. Walsh, illustrated by J. Morrison, University of Queensland Press; 49, Dorothy Dunphy; 12, 13, 'Animals' by Harter, Dover Press; 8, Photographer John Hay, reproduced by kind permission HOUSE & GARDEN; 85, Melbourne Age; 3, 6, 11, 26, 27, 34, 37 (top), 51, 69, 70, 71, Reg Morrison; 41, Nucolorvue Publications Pty. Ltd; 10, 25, 76, 77, 79, 91, Photos-on-File; 19, 47, 54, Promotion Australia; 21, 23, 31, 33 (right) 35, 55, 58, 73, 74, 75, Photos courtesy Qantas CMA The Australian Airline; 22, 23, 'Koobor The Drought Maker' from the painting by Ainslie Roberts; 44, 45, 89, Roland Schicht; 14, By kind co-operation of Royal Botanic Gardens, Kew; 95 (top left), Alma Russell; 24, Photographer Graham Tann for Merehurst; 15, By courtesy of The Trustees of The British Museum (Natural History); 18, 38, 39, J. P. Varin, Jacana; 78, West Australian Newspapers Limited; 92, You Magazine, Mail on Sunday; 29, 30, 50, ZEFA.

65, Goodbye Blinky Bill record and sheet music © Matthews Music Pty. Ltd., P.O. Box 4, Drummoyne, NSW 2047, Australia. Both record and sheet music can be purchased by writing to the above box number.

81, 82, Books by courtesy of the Australian Gift Shop at Western Australia House, 115 Strand, London WC2.

80, Copyright holder Janet Glad gives permission to reproduce illustrations from 'Norman Lindsay's Bears', illustrations Norman Lindsay, published by Macmillan, Melbourne.

81, Copyright holder Janet Glad gives permission to reproduce the cover and inside illustration from 'The Animals Noah Forgot' by A. B. Paterson, illustrations Norman Lindsay, published by Ure Smith, Sydney.

82, The cover pictures from 'The Complete Adventures of Blinky Bill' written and illustrated by Dorothy Wall, and 'Meet Blinky Bill', written by Dorothy Wall and illustrated by Louis Silvestro, are copyright Angus & Robertson Publishers and reprinted with their kind permission.

83, Permission given by John Sands Ltd., for reproduction of the cover of 'Two Thumbs the Koala' by Leslie Rees, illustrator Margaret Senior, Ure Smith, Sydney.

94, Symbols of Australia by Mimmo Cozzolino, published by Penguin Books Australia Ltd.